# Fragmented Waters

Books by Ron Winkler

*Morphosen: Texte* [edition sisyphos, Cologne 2002]
*vereinzelt Passanten: Gedichte* [KOOKbooks, Berlin 2004]
*Fragmentierte Gewässer: Gedichte* [Berlin Verlag, Berlin 2007]
*Frenetische Stille: Gedichte* [Berlin Verlag, Berlin 2010]
*Torp: Prosa* [Verlagshaus J. Frank, Berlin 2010]
*Prachtvolle Mitternacht: Gedichte* [Schöffling & Co., Frankfurt am Main 2013]
*Torp. Neue Wimpern: Prosa* [Verlagshaus J. Frank, Berlin 2013]


As Editor

*Schwerkraft: Junge amerikanische Lyrik* [Jung und Jung, Salzburg 2007]
*Hermetisch offen: Poetiken junger deutschsprachiger AutorInnen*
[Verlagshaus J. Frank, Berlin 2008]
*Neubuch: Neue junge Lyrik* [yedermann Verlag, München 2008]
*Die Schönheit ein deutliches Rauschen: Ostseegedichte*
[Connewitzer Verlagsbuchhandlung, Leipzig 2010]
*Schneegedichte* [Schöffling & Co., Frankfurt am Main 2015]
*Thüringen im Licht: Gedichte aus fünfzig Jahren*
[Wartburg Verlag, Weimar 2015]
*Venedig. Der venezianische Traum: Gedichte*
[Schöffling & Co., Frankfurt am Main 2015]


Translations

*books by*
Sandra Beasley, Billy Collins, Denise Duhamel,
Johannes Frank, Forrest Gander, Arielle Greenberg,
David Lerner, Sarah Manguso, Jeffrey McDaniel,
Matthew Zapruder

Ron Winkler

# Fragmented Waters

*translated
from German
by
Jake Schneider*

Shearsman Books

First published in the United Kingdom in 2016 by
Shearsman Books
50 Westons Hill Drive
Emersons Green
BRISTOL
BS16 7DF

Shearsman Books Ltd Registered Office
30–31 St. James Place, Mangotsfield, Bristol BS16 9JB
*(this address not for correspondence)*

www.shearsman.com

ISBN 978-1-84861-504-5

*Fragmentierte Gewässer* by Ron Winkler
Published by Berlin Verlag, Berlin 2007
© Schöffling & Co. Verlagsbuchhandlung GmbH, Frankfurt am Main
Translations copyright © Jake Schneider, 2016.

This project is supported in part by an award from the
United States National Endowment for the Arts.

ART WORKS.

National
Endowment
for the Arts
arts.gov

# CONTENTS

# little house on the Saale

*for itself*

the sandbox was where we built our first Mount Hyperbole.

we huffed and puffed and kissed it down.

in that chalk circle's co-kingdom, we could still stand

in Heaven and Hell at the same time.

and no one suspected the hackbird.

———

mother was the first variable constant we encountered.

her life an inequation with her husband.

we claimed the pasture as our own private lawn.

for rounds of ramstones, Batman badminton, and so on.

———

apron was a border as porous as twilight.

we could sense kisses behind it like mute crickets

though that quiet cream hardly trickled.

———

I had evangelephant ears on a buzzard head.

maybe I really was an animal pilot.

———

when I prayed through Jehovah's Windows

in that unquantifiable epoch of night,

I'd form an atheist barn with my hands

complete with dream goats, that special milk.

—————————————

now and then we'd settle in for a civic visit.

the *near and dear* relations, our aunts with their hangers-on.

teabirds, we dubbed them. beak streets.

—————————————

those may have been Mercedes-flavored

afternoons of excellence, taken to heart and yet to pen.

until a hand smashed in somewhere. categorical error.

then ruckus, then Pyrrhic silence.

—————————————————

sometimes we'd hand in ideals like model citizens. other times

we were party poopers. played war as the bad guys.

only base stations for the sequel.

# OSMOSIS SOUNDS

## maritime visit diagnostic

all it takes is a glimpse at the water:
either *tango marino* or classic *marinette*.
buoys mark off the iambs of the waves.

~

by all accounts, the colors of the sea
seem overexcitable.

~

yet the water strikes you as rather thin.

~

there's a competition between things. two windswept pines
rivaling for aesthetic inclines.

~

the tide inexhaustible—you could say
it was making payments on a larger debt.

~

the wind stroking the sea like an enthusiastic father.

~

it all gives you a sustainable impression.
even the herons onshore: fishing for relevance.

# by a water neither river nor pond

the wind condemns the trees to a whipping—
a penance obviously full of hot air.

for reassurance, please also note
that the flowers don't bear pistols.

the landscape so dignified that many
a Flemish painter must have lived here.

the grasses in these parts halfway
between hill-swans and bristle-boars.

presumably the trampled greenery
is the flip side of a prudent creature

but the mandatory fauna is something else—
especially the racket faction of the frogs.

when they aren't swimming, they're baptizing
the neighborhood with their throats' green notes.

the waves are unmistakable—
springforms that leap onto shore.

in the *transition area*, a few yards
of mud act as *silt pour l'art*.

the seagulls act on nothing.
their appearance much too disyllabic.

anyone who swims here is no stroke,
but a slash in the water.

## island, overgrown with wind

the sea shone nimble
hydrogen, like bee substrate,
as birds in eyeshot freegulled
on a quest for a calm catch. we noted this
promptly in the log-roll of the wind (details
to be revised later) along with that moment's
water-stems, a handful of madness
for this island overgrown with wind. the hinterland:
a *quintessential rampage zone.*
as much as not.

# in part about fish

as you see it, water is conspicuously
correct, impossible to overtake, and proof
of the liquigevity of fish—
even the way they stare at us
seems professionally primitive although
actual enough, so we side-step them
and start to slurp sibilants (or *sibilantly*)
from clams: that flaccid gourmet
between fish and *gullish*.
needless to say, this correspondence
is a drill, and occasionally a warming
Hosanna. tender as one of those gestures
that hatch in the light unannounced
and come between us by and
large of their own free gill.

# at Island 35

*because of A.P.*

the sea is flawlessly whipped up.
it well deserves a more riveting word.
the wind is going through a pedagogical phase.
the trees stooping down to sheer metaphors.
the wailing wall of the seagull calls implies
a whole wailing settlement behind it.
the concept of a *tide* is probably
particularly appealing to Adventists.
the longer you stare, the frothier.
but that's as tricky to prove
as the kinship between sea-
anemones and animosities.

## reeds of rhetoric

you on the beach, in figurehead pose, confronting a dev-
ocean of water, in the middle of something like foaming,
a moment contaminated with propellant, blurry and therefore
spot-on—the fluttering of froth. that's all for now. this has been
*most sea.* your coast. with salt-service.

## for Hauke Haien

at the edge of a theoretical sea: theoretical sheep,
damming mammals in the white of old teeth. they bit
(*see above*) into green, straw-sipping rectilinear lives.
the wind was classic. the sky
a clear definition. the sun a Sunday.

## picture postcard from a sea

we swam on a slant in the immersive tense
till the towns lost their impact. at least ostensibly,
we dammed coasts in our astonishment. and proposals
to circumvent them. sometimes the sun seemed to be
everything there was. other times things degenerated
into their nouns. apart from that, we'd been having
a time.

## country elegy

this day's transmitter
is tuned to the wind tunnel.

\*

prayer stalks are gaining ground
in the wheat fields.

\*

pollen is dispatched over the land,
*gratuit* et *libre*.

\*

the flowers retrieve flagrant
aromas from inventory.

\*

lone gusts incite gnarled shrubs
to branching hymns.

\*

inside some bellflowers,
church attempts are swinging.

\*

as always, the cats businesslike
with their surroundings.

*

the birds are overruled. they conclude
the day in *silent mode.*

*

at midnight comes the regional
anthem of frogs around the pond.

## telegram from a sea

the shoreline: more or less
borderland. the water: articulate enough.
the waves: free radicals.

## autumn telegram

the trees: inadvertent birdbrackets

the crows: pitchblack tendencies

the fruit: regrettably mis-taken

## backwater, trance style

black-and-white cows like color bloopers on a pasture

taking turns soundchecking their fantastic samples

swallows overhead: pointy-cornered float-hooks

cottonwoods behind the scenes supply summer snow

here and there fugues with no plot at all

like *shyness*

and maybe to mention the weather: *warmplay*


everything almost lines up with its critical reading

the stinging nettle families of pain reservoirs

the light very *Klopstock*

other superlatives are still ripening

though we almost expect it

*the care with which the rain is wrong*

## for a village in the shade of the Elbe

there are two types of *stork* here.
the *frog* form of existence works a sound unit.
which grates the ear but runs all right.
the different editions of *cat* run worse.
this is no catwalk. here horses are hitching
for attention. and cheeping wrens wake up
re-cast as peeping toms.

## heat (Hitzacker)

on the horizon: gallweather, thunderheather—
the jackdaws deep, a jackyawn beneath, perceptible
and gaping, and in my haste I left behind a *chaos
shadow* like auxiliary noises
for the upcoming hedge (etc.) purge.
which hardly *partitioned.* every second pressed
on the barometer, and when you said (something
to the effect of) *Heaven is my favorite bar,*
voices of sorts bubbled up
on by: skylarks, groundlaughter.

## wasp coat

I recommend holding an ear up to summer,
that heated pollen bestowal, nestified
with insect islands, which I see as utmost *wasp coat*,
a buzzing *phonographed* into the air, sometimes
all too remarkable when a *bribery sting*
inspires the skin to a long-lasting song.

## the poem has been drinking

for one thing, the present tense of May bugs, that stagger
in the tunics of friendly tanned monks. and
since it's May, also the canola, entire fields,
entire olfactory landscapes, oily and insipid,
but intrusively yellow, virtually *overcolored.*
(not me—the poem.) during a stork break,
the birds sow even more enunciated chirps. stalked
by the caution of the resident cats.
that's just the way it goes. like the bats
after dark: simple *skinned flight.*
the poem partook of *cow,* too,
breathalizably.

*for Friederike von Koenigswald*

## all set swimming pool

the low noise of osmosis,
and the wave gardener with its sailor gestures,
and the balanced scale between relaxing
and a sunburn,
and the hydronauts who set up camp on white flags
    to bring themselves a dry peace,
and the shadowy homeland of a cool glass of conversation,
and the second-hand chorus of chlorine,
and the hitched teams of oil-spreading fingers,
and the azure and green audience hall of a quick-to-drip-off
    artificial sea,
and your ache for sustainable swimming,
and the Magellanic cloud of silence, right
    before the dive into water.

# SUNDAYS IN HASTY NAKEDNESS

# altitude training, dog story

*for Renatus Deckert*

morning was a bygone dog,
a cloud in a chase with wind—

the early, industrious altitude training
of ambitious water.

and summer joined in with swallow thunderstorms,
the arcs of a furious species—

so inconsequential you had to marvel. hardly
room between them for sky.

    ×

I love to summon goose prairies on a woman's skin
and contemplate how close to that a poem
can approach.

    ×

all these museums, often open until someone notices.

box seats that shoot out swallows for no more
than several summers.

    ×

for several summers I donated acorns to the evergreen forest.
*boar desserts.* my yet-dog held
onto their smell for a while.

there were so many clouds, so much canine patience, so
few truffles.

                    ×


the invention of the *kennel* method: back then
I hardly suspected its reach. we learned loyally: a comma
always belongs between two subordinate countries.

                    ×


at noon the relay race of church
bells. homeland can be so innocuous.

                    ×


grandmother's piercing came from a dreamed birthplace.
years after she died. in her navel.
but it didn't bring her any nearer to me.

every other sleep is a fright train.
the hand-me-down cities of days. out of control
like the provoking corners in school.

at times I appreciate that. the impressions
approaching the words up close. so as not to be a hindrance.

                    ×

later no clouds left. you could go crazy
in there. in the evening, light delivers
a lecture on darkness. it is well received.

×

I still haven't departed from myself. I am fleshed
out, and sometimes have reflexes
back to some kind of yesterday:

involuntary souvenirs, troves of sighs. as prolonged
as stenographic transcripts of fluttering eyelids.

×

in one of them I am standing, parted on the side.
ready for a rebuke. my cheeks red as
the crutches distributed in my
essays… *Yours in Socialism.*

×

it fits in the nature of things that metaphors bloom
in them. for millennia this mode has kept *moon*
describable.

×

nothing not to the reach of the lexical. as a paradigm
grandfather's beer consumption. every trip to KONSUM
a galaxy of symbols (Gagarin).

but there was more than that. we would *go cherry*
picking and kiss. sometimes one another.

this chapter has rarely been left out.
*love*. lotus studies on a foreign body. instilling
in it the desire to be a flavor.

     ×

memory knits a scarf in my head.
the material bunched in a corner as if it had a cold.

yet consciousness is the worst
at listening. its ear is the monitor of thousands of symbols.

it had quickly made me telesomatic. into
a swallowlike being
with a flightpath wandering off its own course.

     ×

appeals were rarely fruitful,
unlike apple blossoms. father's pride, brought up
as cellar kids

with cheeks like goodwill: balled-up summer
that we stuck in our bags—

knapsacks that shrugged with our shoulders,
one step low tide, the next step high.

     ×

Eden plans alternating
with the needs of the *Faculty of Contemporary Studies*,
which you had to take in sips.

             ×


but there were also
several Furies there, in the library,
just in case.

and swallows: birds on the run
who've been forming waves over rooftops for ages.

in *honest black and white*, which took color
from day, but brought movement.

and mother's movement waved back
through a practically intact family's
underclothes, drying on the line.

             ×


intimacy started just out the front door. many lost it
as easily as house keys
and never returned.

still there are usually back doors: neuroses and that language
in the blue-screen method… for a world as will
and water vapor.

             ××

most types of behavior
are out of natural enemies.

xx

I feel *dog.* chew patiently on the tough meat
of perception.

x

father was the master at dismantling erstwhile animals.
top-grade creatures of utility.

their last hike led them over the counter onto plates.
their *Stairway to Heaven* the inner graveyard
of floral bags.

x

I couldn't draw any of it. not the churches,
nor any of the cherry chapters: the sweet supporting capitals
of a life absorbed so *spatially.*

not mother's kitchen. not grandmother's dialect.
not my adrenaline rush after deliberately destroying

something that refused to be drawn—that you could
only pad with opinions.

with nearly intact clouds. that final layer
under which the weather (or weathers) rumbled

and trees became instruments in the wind, branch by branch,
limb by limb.

×

we liked to picnic at the edge
of their improvisations. viewed from outside, a small prop room
of sounds, motions, hairstyles.

××

we offered ourselves to the landscape.
we, the strange of nature.

××

every note my father listened to in that life
was a brass player.

×

*so much depends / upon* music. my greatest love
grew out of a concert.

brass players were denied admittance.
only the altitude training of the violins, their goose prairies
in a bowed minor key.

then the first kiss—a Bartók ballet.
the last one will come at the close of a still unfinished symphony

where there are unlikely to be any season brochures

or any parachutes whose strings I could pull off:
*it haunts me... it haunts me not...*

                ×


always the manhunt for pictures, and the incidental
one for picture frames. between the two,

the head that struggled to raise itself up
yet never lost interest.

                ×


*limestone barn*, I say. crammed full
of me, my refutation. that magical atavism.

day after day I dance there with the bizarre evolutions
of a handful of thoughts.

mother would have described that differently. or
tacitly slipped pocket money to idiocy.
(*...for swallows*)

I could ask her for some. but she doesn't exist that way.
and the dog of this vision
looks out so gently.

                ×


that's what he trained so hard for.

## photograph mealtimes

silver dishes were Sunday's
bridle; out of the kitchen
came steaming platters, out of love
napkins; nothing as close to us
as the table that ensured our
persistence, hands folded under
it in a rumbling Our Hunger;
authentic barn meat, *pure breast*;
and to top it off, we rolled up our
sleeves for some *private plums*
after mostly People's potatoes:
a sentence was never peeled so
clean, even if the conversations
shimmered like the photograph—
father in his best years,
never in the end to keep off
the bitters of an exhaustion
that seemed rented from owls.

## antler archive

my parents frequently flipped open
the book of quiet conflict. usually
if that happened I'd go walk one of
my childhood's three dogs.
they'd yowl whole utopias together.
sister played grandmother and had
bad hearing. grandmother herself heard fine,
but might as well have been on permanent vacation
in the world of the waltz. by then grandfather
was his own calm book. we'd read it
together out of photo albums. those were afternoons
heavy and full of smoke like the brocade curtains
in the *good parlor*. kale green with gold
edging: every guest praised the choice, then the liqueur.
visits were *Tours de la Paix*. you'd practice
philanthropy and freedom: here antlers played
the role of the Chairman on the wall.
after school, consciousness began
as a test pattern (*channel two*). it was soothing
when sister was dying one of her pimple deaths
or grandmother had geared up the turntable
to a tango. I reaped pocket change
from her for my patience, and pralines.
at first I detested them all. later they were
the sweet local branches of the family tree.
they made my tongue escape.

# sideroom

the past that loved me:
inceptions of lines, interceptions
of classes. like Civics.
or Sundays in hasty nakedness:
we'd take the stipulated baths
rigorously enough for export.
a pair of mother's eyes rinsed
you for inspection. a love
like a Bathtub Bureau that
allotted time and also religion,
when the moment struck.
which was the case not unoften.
this offered me scant protection
from sociopathic dreams. at least sleep
was neutral about ideology.
the demons there wore no
Uncle Joe moustaches, wore
only my fear in their
unauthorized sublets
of rooms. I myself seemed
to be a sideroom,
a mistibule where
others teach local history.
but that only made me hurt, later
*sorry*. and the cortical
climate knows greater
pains. even by name. even by
pen name. there was my toothache,
and there was the categorical

imperfect of an unclear youth.
peach fuzz over my lips. inside
my eyes, a peacock that stayed
undefined. you were never
the milk monitor, and if you ever
were, then in the footnote zone, so
everyone could move
on. as a ceremony, etc.
and eventually walk down the
cereal aisle. right at you.

# HARES, THEIR OWN
# FORM OF GOVERNMENT

## journal, Lago Momentane

our arrival was catastrophically lovely,
the sky scenically colorless, and the present
like a precise body of water.
we collected gods and polished
them late into the night. the air was
big. there were chanted animals,
apparitions with idiosyncratic panicles.
most of it looked possible.
we felt strikingly *now*.

## Provence, *Place du Marché*

the olive mongers wouldn't admit to dealing in universes.

around the oranges, though, they were proud of it.

nothing but a cover for a bitter childhood.

some of the stands' fishitude stood out.

so many sea creatures had reached a *Mont Blanc*.

their chill called to us in French—deceptively.

after storming past the butchers' barricades,

we took a break on the rounds of the melons. for a spare coin

you could get *fleurs du malheur.*

# a stroll in Suffolk

*probably for A. and M.*

the ponds we saw were connected by swans
to the sea. their screams walked right in
without knocking (and weren't white either).

we ate apples on dew—that's how we understood autumn,
the skin of things dissolving, an early hint of November (debit),
half lingering summer (credit).

the leaves had lost some poise. the wind assigned
them to feet. it all went downhill.

a smatter of (almost awkward) stags withdrew grass from a clearing.
we identified them, on a hunch, as *upstanding carpet gleaners.*

the hares (think: *rabbits*), which we could
scare up brown, had their own form of government.
they indicated directions (as vectors).
we thought that made an interesting math problem,
but soon subtracted ourselves from the equation.

a few miles later we spotted the sea.
an offshoot of a great big color.

# Giza Mon Amour

*for Christiane Wohlrab*

the pyramids seem
lifted from a textbook on aesthetics.
hawkers swoop in with vocabulary
for withstanding their beauty.
the hieroglyph for stoicism
must be a camel.
pretty soon everyone succumbs
to the heliopuncture of the sun.
to see other old gods, there's
an entrance fee. the Sphinx
has been known to convey
a rather inaccurate picture.

# bamboo winter, Paris

it was more than *touristy*
the way you laid shadows in Montmartre,
incessant crucivisitor at *Place Sacré Coeur*,
in the robes of a sacred, atheist gesture...

you said it lacked for height, multiple layers
of springtime, that and what you called
*home linguistics*, which was just as wrong
as your recap for that garçon:
*I had the snow*—can we pay please?—and with a
gulp: bitten-off language.

then we tossed the tip to the guys
sipping Saint Pigalle with their dogs
for the smell of endearment in the streets,
akin to wax and dish soap,
that rinsed around your one-lane
show, right on target, but

harder to substantiate
than our renewable, Sahel-colored impression
of the city in one of its bamboo winters,
where you harvested walking sticks
for cobweb days.

## so Paris

you said that this city derived etymologically from paradise.
or parasite.
that on many days the Seine was a sign of being.
but sometimes only of boats.
on the axes of duty, commuters made the streets vibrate
with their brand of accidental cartography.
outside multiple churches, we confronted Catholic patience.
then waited our turn for monalisality and Eiffel metal.
we later determined the date by the
number of burning cars.
we knew the reason. the time was now.

## altar inclination

the way I knew you, as a chant from naked fragrant June,
and the way you could hasten your hair, was a trip
to a southern condition. there were four-lipped coasts there,
the touch of acacia, and in the dunes behind them we exchanged
unusual light, an almost genetic correspondence
that we called an altar and where we deposited deep sea nights,
little jellyfish sensualities under the auspices
of our eye bugs and sometimes our heron joints.
I researched in you the most fantastical metaphors
of this century and tended to the feral zoo
of your glances. we oystered around each other oceanically, as
we belonged among those who had shamanic dreams
and those who are dreamt of shamanically. I was
never so two as with you.

## atlas of stings

for years you'd logged your mosquito bites
on a dressmaker's dummy.

because nothing could be *only* chance,
everything has a pattern or, to put it non-
mechanically: a god at the ready.

and in light of that pattern, your atlas of stings
is at last an irrefutable world of its own.

# DANCE FICTION

## a day like december

this day has glacial tendencies.

how could it be any different, with winter underlying it?

the cloud's envelope goes unopened.

although that delivery deeply involves me, *par avion*.

the sky works for the grayscale sector.

a new color scheme seems to be prevailing: dietary light.

at least the sun keeps up appearances.

the poplars a Mohawk on the horizon.

even now the boulevards lead to the labial.

they too are dotted by snowfall.

what fell before could pass for a petticoat.

the landscape hasn't been that landscapelike for ages.

which reminds me of another thing:

a few ponds award themselves to the woods as glassy medals.

but the birds' warm flurries bluff

that all away.

## case study: *rain*

we considered the fragmented waters a phenomenon
between the adjectives *light* and *tempestuous*.

it never rained only once per rain.

sometimes we felt hormones steering towards us.

other times: palpable antonyms for *desert*.

we felt that the rain was the most drinkable weather.

was *hydrogenity*.

it rained mostly away from the universe.

and towards the universe.

oceans sliding past over our heads. time capsules
filled with themselves.

dating back to the first hour.

## clouds

essentially nothing. then again a Jehovah-colored *barely.*

the make-it-look-easy depiction of a wetness. *under the influence of water.*

essentially nothing. only unspectacular regions of the spectrum

smuggled straight across the sky. vague spheres and meta-

spheres. essentially nothing. now and then

serving as a cyclical permutation of a purported connection.

quiet playlists in the tab stops of *wind.*

showrooms like the space in between. essentially nothing.

eventually concluding in output from something

that stands to reason. return.

# surrounding schnee

*for J.S., R.H. and M.R.*

we love this cold fractal grammar.

the small-boned teetering of snow in the air.

the complex sashaying of small-boned snow
through the atmosphere.

the uncharted territory outside our eyes' white boxes.
a simplified take on the surroundings.

we love these soundless hoofbeats at the start
of *it's sticking.*

we love these complicated intensive care units
of specific climactic conditions.

their unobtrusive complication.

the concreteness of *specific imbalance.*

we love the auto-verifying turbulence.

and the phenomenon itself (as a memory
of that phenomenon.)

with caution, we love the peaceful *overbombing.*

and later the slinking constructivism
of a white Sanskrit on top of things.

# an equadorial

the rainforest was a liquid.
the greenery a substance. we dreamt of dehydration.

the mosquitos we called *beastly chili peppers*
seemed like macrobiological consequences of quantum
        sting theory.
gentleness dripped from the trees.

we learned to purge the guanine
from our vision (dreaming of *simple dimensional analysis*).
it all felt so nucleotidal, so liberating.

stray photon packets
glided on the ground like *dance fiction*.
we dreamt of snowiness.

the wild ceiling fans overhead reminded us of hummingbirds.
they were today's quickest quiet.
we had nightmares about what else carbon had in the cards.

for hours the same shifting image
of very polygonal vegetation. the heat was despotic.
we dreamt of it for ages.

the genetic aspects of the landscape had biomorphic features.
in comparison we felt practically inanimate.
we dreamt of the Tarzanity of our existence.

sometimes matter changed our course.
usually a carnivore reservoir.
we dreamt of a recording studio à la Noah.

when wind erupted, we could tell the Big Bang was withdrawing.
that's where we halted. only the language kept going.

# HALF-DATA

## worldview, to go

forest is a nice kind of agglutination.

the trees, for instance, tend to branch off

perfectly but seem natural anyway.

now and then something twitches between twigs.

usually an object or a type

of idyllic information. a winged space

with the potential to be substantially correct.

*I can burn it for you, no problem.*

## field guide for eco-tourists

the blossoms put their stamp on the air.

the wind is one of the connectors.

the trees are leafleteers. their branches seem stilted.

the birds can be identified as Winded Migration.

the hares as fright. something exists

beyond the flatscreen of a lake. it could be fundamental.

some animals are grazing on a surface.

maybe they're for real.

something old is sinking on the horizon.

## sweet home lambs

you were positive that the truth of these spaces
was greater than wool, that their fluffy wading
spread through great distances was a longing
to be translated: into something less oxygenated
maybe. or maybe not. maybe
they want to be a kind of distance from themselves
(the species *distance from themselves*).
if they were Capitalism, they could sell *everything*
only the fence would need to be reorganized.

## pen insula

autumn grew gradually out of overblown dunes.

we were there, engulfed by Pollock weather.

the waves—a sea held sway—fell back on lots of water.

moisture could erupt at any moment.

we took fish for a strange breath ingredient.

the trelliswork of the trees culminated in fruit.

other, mobile containers looked human.

which was merely contingent on the outdoors.

# high-end experience

the morning alternated between extradition

of atheism and hasty Catholicization.

the sunbeams radiated modernity. they evaded

an explicit message. on that note,

behind some terms I extrapolated trees.

"may he not google himself away—

in this sharply subsiding forest."

not every ellipsis in there was a gap. but almost.

along the way, a third party happened to trample the updates

of several grasses. they could have been beta versions.

although the sky's bankrupt cloud cover drew my attention

away.

## animalated poem

you should have conceded that off the bat, rock climb meadows
like schisms between dead-serious peaks (*Mountains
of Matter*). under the wasp of the light, something
antlered into view—almost a total—facing us, an opaque
pelt of movement. we wished we could pet these facts
of the matter, their peels that seemed distinct from freedom
in the Marlboro sense of the word. in a flash of Bambilosophy,
we suspected deer decoys—or some similar kind
of *countryside trash*. ultimately we were too participial
to be integrated into these tag clouds. besides it was awfully
brisk here at Lake Nonsense—about ten Derrida.

## that certain sense of here

obviously *garages*. and rental quasars. there was us
and the flora alerts in between. the towns pointed
the wrong way. the days were still getting by,
the nights slept right through us.
where there was a will, there was a wheezing ground. castanet
alleys and—practically in stereo—the insinuation
of semantic surf. that passed in some circles
for rhetoric, in others for indeterminate reeds.
these lingua flora converted conditions into something like colors.
*dangerous couplings* or mind-expanding tropes.
we gladly settled down in this *range of signifiers*.
and cautiously herded the lone sheep of the righteous.

## Palm Beach

we came here for the cupped hand
      beaches
and the waves that went beyond our
      requirements.
the sea shone like an oracle prophesying
      water.
on second glance, some of the pontoons were only
      swans.
above us, seagulls were conjugated by entirely different
      seagulls.
the palms dangled their latest crop rotation: planetoids swaddled
      in green.
they were supposed to be escape pods. but of course that
      went straight
to our download habits. the grains of sand, like eager
      apostles,
trailed us for several more weeks. cities and
      fields
and an assortment
      of other folders shimmered with heat on the horizon.
it was a decent compilation.

## souvenir drive

*for Jan Wagner*

behind the copious sheep were the premium highlands.
the alpha landscape was unmistakable,
a suitable design: tectonic middle tier
in its best years. you brought up
cooperative *mountaineering*, then, a few egotistical pubs later,
the manic harvest. who knew.
this foreignness was an intransitive
homeland—and therefore dangerous. you kept malt cows
who acted like malt cows. every day
contained about ten kilograms of beauty.
sunrises like monsoons. precipitation sometimes
like light, sometimes like nouns.
quote unquote Glenn Gould birds all around us. peculiar
windows. based on the same charter language.
a bridge over something missing.
the way you looked back at them on your departure
was oddly Victorian.

## organism garden

here, the circumstances held out their nominatives in our direction.
       avenues cultivated incidental (maple) trees.
the lawn was a moratorium. we
       had *taken a shine*, oblivious to the background, clearly
escorted by alleged bees—
       complete with their opportune attributes.
the other multicellular organisms' features elicited the requisite
         hyperlatives from us.
       we'd figured that in. how lovely,
the gentle dose of deer motifs at the outskirts
       of this park. *discrete portions* on the way
from truth to reality.
       and so helpfully helpless.

# zoological waiting

*without Hannah Arendt*

*simple future.* it had to do with cumulative biochemistry in the
        form of observation.
afternoons like foreign animals
        that flipped open their explicable eyes like accessories
or love. *present imperative passive.* that was
        peak usage
and quickly concocted. sugar, placebo, and a bit
        of that psychic freight.
*territorial preterite* or rather *downunder light.*
        we gave ourselves the gift of fully
        convertible bonnet-bee software. locust gestures.
anyway, entire objects. *perfect:*
        nanomoments. teabag childhood. pictures of remarkable
offspring: engineers of the filth that built circuits
        on the beach out of integrated sand.
(*vita fragila*). foul-sounding wasps there instructed their enemies
        on the concept of a ruthless indicative.

## deer meter

out of a prepared decoy landscape we extracted
    a part of the borough:
a typical out-of-focus population of deer.
we plunged a homeopathic sample of them
    into our synaptic solution
and ascertained that their forest function
had an inversely reciprocal relationship
    with the trees, or at least behaved as such
    (→Schrödinger flickering).
their frequency was foliage, their median far above zero.
    they could be quantified with chromology and clocks.
we divided a few of the specimens into scaffolding, sounds,
and spatialities
(as for me, most of all I liked the eyes, whose
values were inconclusive).
we categorized them as packages of parallel impulses
    with fluctuating locations. they over-coupled each other and
had interrelated
spellings. their decelerated evolution gave us time.
so we abandoned them to radial decay and calmly went
    back to our apartment products.

# the extent of deer

from an artificially generated landscape of enticement, we selected
a mild enclave: a population of distinctively insecure deer.
intending homeopathy, we submerged them
    in our synaptic brine,
finding that the trend of their wooden momentum
ran, or better, appeared to run
    inversely proportional
    to that of the trees (=Schrödinger flare).
our sample's frequency was naiveté,
its substance a positive number which could be measured following
    theories of colors and clocks.
we dismantled several pieces into enclosures, audio,
and geometry
(I went for the eyes, which didn't
encapsulate anything).
then we classified them as parcels of steadily improving instincts
    with variable bonding. they copulated amongst themselves and
likewise displayed great similarities
in orthography. their evolution was approaching the limit: to our
advantage. so we reverse-engineered them and headed home
    to sleeker things.

*[the German original was based on an
earlier English translation of the preceding poem]*

## never alps

*for Steffen Popp*

which was a more decisive mood indicator,
        the snow caribou
        or
the caribou snow? the former saw like a free-form haiku,
        the latter looked
        like one.
out of the mountains' milk cliff, the avalanche
        dogs foamed up
        step by step.
they were serviceable as objects (of our understanding).
        their eyes boded
        law and valley.
purely for their own safety, we filed
        their biometric data
        away—
and set up a subdomain: *files of fur*. this too
        occurred
        by means of Columbus.
the highest estimated alpine pastures could
        almost shake themselves loose
        from the natural term.
they were composed of clear definitions. these
        *items*
        alone made the way up worth it.

## sea sponges

from afar, their colony resembled an amalgamation
of clenched fists. fish
browsed about them: slim speechless
shapes. the sponges—
which felt like the gloves
we were wearing—
still bathed just for themselves.
their innards instructions for journeys
*to the center of the earth.*
we touched them like they were monuments
against their use as cleaning implements.
we liked their adorable apathy.
so we took a few along, to share
our evolution with theirs.

# x-referential field portrait

so these cows, right, were parading
around like absurd typewriters.
for that matter they weren't cows at all.
more like black-and-white moments caught in pixels.
and no typewriter could muck up
a meadow. whatever. what mattered
was the blink-of-an-eye-ness of a thing.
together with airy psyche, right.
multiple dimensions bottomed against each other
and, in spite of constant refreshing, turned up
tainted search results: grass droplets,
existence deposits,
and past them the migration
of a narrow awareness. here
the meadow and there the contorted messages
of their horns. eyes
like uninhabited planets. cows, right,
as agreed upon, cows—
at the end of their biography.

## untitled

look, those layers without generators, those *magnetic meadows*
  as if built for us
and us alone, *bees of consciousness* in the freeware
  of light, which runs
antler-like behind its relativistic backdrop.

never forget—since the language put us here—
  to swallow the chatroom of your pride
and report on us in butterflies, to insist that we
  be or are the *quaking bog*
between slept and sleeped. existences softly *smeared
  into each other.*

observe us with the C-14 technique. we are taking pains
  to get a correct echo.
of course we are swaddled in animals *(friendly hired)*
  and not always properly metered.
still, measure us by environment,
  not theory.

don't make yourself at home in us. be my guest
  and rest assured, that is more than a word. we are new
in some definitions, but here we are nimble.
  and so forth.

# Translator's Note

A word, in a Ron Winkler poem, is a double agent. Upon closer inspection, it might well be riffing on an Eastern Bloc bicycle race or a Gertrude Stein poem or a French documentary about birds. Its second identity might not be stable (not even in Ron's own conception, as I've learned in asking him about these poems over ten years), and it will almost certainly be camouflaged in the German jungle of multi-noun mash-ups.

In the opening poem, for instance, the speaker has "Segensohren an einem Igelschädel." Literally, that translates as "blessing-ears on a hedgehog-skull." A pleasant absurdity with no steady handholds. In fact, Winkler is playing on *Segelohren*, or "sail-ears," a childhood insult for the aurally well-endowed; the *Igel* (hedgehog) hairstyle is just a buzz cut. My translation: "I had evangelephant ears on a buzzard head." I've fitted in the religion and the animal, but not the literal meaning.

To compensate for the instances where a pun or neologism was lost in translation, the English versions gained an occasional coinage of their own. For example, lacking an equivalent for the German *Promille*, the common unit for blood-alcohol concentration, I found a new Winkleresque adverb for roadside inebriation tests: "breathalizably."

These poems notice the nature in human nature and likewise anthropomorphize the woods. The hares have their "own form of government." And yes, the species of Ron's swallows and seagulls are important, but so are the puns and idioms by which he repurposes them. Sometimes, as with the hedgehog above, I had to call in a biological understudy, neglecting the chirp of grudge-bearing crickets to invent "bonnet-bee software" or making the original revolver-leaves—a German term for tabloids—bloom in the line "their flowers don't bear pistols."

The true identities of the exuberant words and wildlife may defy definition. It's my hope that you can see Ron's forest for my translated trees.

www.ingramcontent.com/pod-product-compliance
Lightning Source LLC
Chambersburg PA
CBHW031928080426
42734CB00007B/590